Twenty

Shyanna Mutz

ISBN: 9798687625104

to the boy who changed my life,
thank you for not loving me so
I could learn to love myself.

to anyone who feels alone in their journey.
let this be a reminder that you are not.

Introduction

The day I turned twenty, I jumped out of a plane.

I did this to kickstart what would hopefully be one of the best years of my life. It was the start of my twenties and my head was swirling with all of the possibilities that come with entering this chapter of life. when I jumped from the plane, I never thought that I'd hit rock bottom that year. It seemed as though my mental health was plummeting with every month that passed. Don't get me wrong, I was excelling in my classes, still doing things I enjoyed and having fun at school. But some days, this was the opposite. Some days, I woke up with a genuine desire to leave this earth. I couldn't explain where it was coming from, it was just there. With days like this happening more and more, my anxiety and self worth was dwindling. I was searching for anyone or anything that would give me validation. That's when I met him. And that's when my life went off the rails in every good and bad way. Suddenly, everything was about making him happy to avoid the struggles I faced myself. If I was focusing all my energy onto one person, there was no room for me to think about how scared I was regarding my own mental health. The relationship got intense extremely fast and so did my feelings for him. It also ended extremely fast, too. I was devastated. Not only had I lost him, but I lost myself. And so began my journey of self care. I absolutely hated that term at first, but I've learned that it is one of the best practices a person can do in their life. Through this self care journey, I have learned to value myself, have patience and to not undermine small accomplishments. Most importantly, I learned that I am bipolar, which was the biggest puzzle piece missing in my life. It took multiple medications and multiple breakdowns, but I finally was able to put a label on the something that scared me for so many years. When I received the diagnosis, it was like I put on a pair of glasses. Everything made more sense. Twenty also brought a pandemic and a social movement in a matter of a few months. These two events have drastically changed the world we live in but also the way that I now live my personal life.

After getting through the toughest part of the healing process, I decided I wanted something I could physically hold as a reminder of this life changing year. And so, the making of this book began. I have been writing poems for this book since early January of 2019 and decided to compile them into a book in the summer of 2020. I wrote these poems during manic episodes as well as during my worst depressive episodes. Writing is truly what got me through the deepest hurt that I have ever experienced. It made me feel present. It helped me stay alive. The poems in this book are intentionally placed to tell a story of my twentieth year from start to finish. It introduces characters and narrates side plots that all come together in the end. I hope that as the reader, you will be able to see this story unfold with every page you turn.

My twentieth year was nothing like I expected. It was full of firsts, self discovery, falling in and out of love, mourning, healing and growth. It was hell at times, but I was brave enough to change the path I was going down. It wasn't until this year that I realized how much work needed to be done on my life and I am still continuing that work. I am finally growing into the woman who I can look at in the mirror and be proud of. I wish I could tell you that this year was everything I thought it would be, but this could not be farther from the truth;

It was messy and ugly and complex and scary and so
incredibly beautiful.

This is that story.

"Let everything happen to you: beauty and terror. Just keep going. No feeling is final.
- Rainer Maria Rilke

on writing

I write to feel something,
anything to take the pain away
and down on paper so it
leaves my head long
enough to write again.

firsts

twenty took my innocence
when I stopped waiting
for fear to make the first move.
that's when I found myself
falling from planes and
falling in love,
kissing on park benches and
sleeping with him too,
piercing my nose and
smoking on porches,
seeking help to save my life and
starting over with fear on my side
and not in front on me.

from the ground

six feet seems shallow

compared to the depths

my thoughts take me to,

so it doesn't scare me

to think maybe I

don't belong here and

maybe

I don't want to be either.

San Antonio to Huntsville to San Antonio
to Huntsville to

my heart stretches over

212 miles of road,

through the bark of pine trees,

past small texas towns

and across a southern sky.

I fill the backseat with demons

that follow me back and forth

between the two cities;

they remind me coming

home is awful but so is going back.

I really do try to enjoy the long drive.

I have friends in both places,

good and bad memories

and favorite places to eat,

just like any destination you

travel to in life so

why is it so hard to want to live in either?
most times it's hard to want to live at all.

the poet

the room was crowded,

but for her it was just the two of them.

a spotlight was cast upon him as he read from the stage,

everything else faded to grain and murmurs.

she listened intently as his lips spoke

of heartbreak and headaches.

her eyes followed his hands as they moved from his

pockets to his hips.

his words were not for her,

but they tapped her heart.

he stepped off the stage,

still remaining on her mind.

his glow traveled with him,

striking her with a subtle glance as he found his seat.

applause and taps on glass brought her back,

she wasn't the only one listening.

his hands now grasped his drink;

his lips echoed laughs.

the room was crowded

but she was lost in her head,

where his hands held her face

and his lips embraced hers.

the girl

this poem isn't about me
because it describes a girl who doesn't hurt
and believes she deserves the world.
it's about a girl that never cries over boys
but only laughs because they look funny
when they walk away.
this girl stares fear in the eyes
and makes it shy from her glare.
it's for a girl who takes walks for fun and not
to forget about the writing on the wall.
this isn't about me but it's about the girl
who I've ran next to for years but I'm
the one that trips over the bumps.

the adventures of two broken bodies
seeking romance at the worst time

late nights and long drives
touching at midnight and
laughter during love.

singing in cars,
smoking at sunrise,
watching films on weekends
and fighting on weekdays.

meeting families
making mistakes
chasing the thrill and
running from the truth.

digging graves and
falling in too fast
feeling for a way out
and finding no excuse.

meeting in the middle
to accept this won't work

and mourning what could have been

if we were made for each other.

body language

the truth was lost in between the sheets
we entangled ourselves in and
you knew where to find it but
the search stopped when
my legs were open and your head
was filled with ways to make me moan.

the truth was on the tip of your tongue
but only when it wasn't in my mouth;
spreading lies around the inside of my cheeks
that tasted too good to notice.

we both knew the truth that stood
as bare as our chests when they met in your bed
but we ignored what would end our intimate nights-
the truth that you liked to feel me
but you didn't feel the same way.

I can't take her anywhere

I felt it coming the moment I left my house.
please don't do this. not today. please.
the sinking starting halfway to my destination
and I could feel myself leaving the moment
to surrender to the thoughts in my head.
no. it's not real. focus on what's in front of you.
I did everything I could;
blared music, bit my tongue, grasped
the steering wheel until my knuckles turned white.
snap out of it. they can't see this side of you.
but it was too late.
I accepted my fate of feeling lifeless;
like every move was through molasses,
like life was pointless until further notice.
why do you always do this.
I turned around to go back home and
retreated to my bed where I knew the
monster that feeds on my feelings couldn't find me.
sleep this off. sleep until you feel safe.
when will I feel safe?

at least he looks cool

he only loves me after hours,

when his friends have gone home

and he talks in circles when I

ask him what we are,

but at least he plays guitar at

parties and while everyone gets high

he charms the girls and boys with his big brain

and I watch from the crowd thinking,

"at least I know he'll be mine later tonight."

on most occasions,

he makes me feel like I'm not enough

because I lack his confidence to dance

like no one is watching;

he only likes how I move when he

wants my body and quite frankly,

I'm fully aware that he is going to break by heart,

probably in his denim jacket and the shoes he skates in,

but at least he'll look cool doing it.

what it feels like to not be loved back

the feeling is somewhat indescribable
because there is no pain that feels quite like it
but I can imagine it feels like a bullet in the form of
words striking the chest and piercing innocent flesh
with an intensity so strong that the earth shakes as the
heart erupts.

it feels like jumping from an aircraft without a parachute
thinking you'll make it anyways but you don't.
it feels like being tossed in the ocean with chains around
your ankles and the key is in the pocket of his jeans.

it feels like your world has been set on fire
and the flames run through your veins and engulf every
ounce of your body and you scream to make the torture
stop but the blaze burns brighter until your eyes match
the embers of your torched city.

it feels like leaving the scene of a wreck with a broken
smile because you doubt you'll ever be happy again.

all the ways to say best friend

other half/ best bud/ dance partner/ second self/ sister/ soulmate/ first one to the scene/ first one to know everything/ concert buddy/ friend for life/ I'd be lost without you/ coffee date/ calls at 3 AM/ fighting for no reason/ riding home separate after the football game/ realizing how stupid we're acting/ laughing till our stomachs hurt/ crushing on the same boy / "act cool, he's walking our way"/ growing up together/ around for every holiday/ our little sisters have sleepovers/ our parents know each other's names/ borrowing clothes/ you're nothing like me in the best ways/ I need you to keep me sane/ come over unannounced/ come as you are/ even though you'll probably be a little late/ unconditional/ listens to every complaint/ tells the honest truth/ brings ice cream after a breakup/ love you in case I die/ but you better not die before me/ I'm so glad I ran into you at camp/ my life has never been the same/ let's keep making memories/ I love you/ Jazmin

living history

we are walking relics;
artifacts dressed in designer clothes
moving through time as we witness
the worst case scenarios happen
right in front of us.

we remember where we were
when disease locked us away;
when the world froze and all
we could do was watch from the window.

we cry when reminded of
the riots that made us break free;
when the call for change was stronger
than the order to stay home.

we were made to endure these hardships;
to survive the coldest treatment in order
to write it down and save it for later.
we were made human to make history.

we are stitched into the narrative

of this nation;

a narrative that cannot be erased.

we stand today to prove that we

are the past-

and it's alive and breathing

even when it gets knocked down.

the dissatisfaction of being human

it's not easy to admit that I'm not okay,
that I spend half the day pacing
back and forth just to feel like I
have a purpose here.

maybe if I'm moving,
my mind will focus on the
patterns I make in the floor
and not on the rapid thoughts
that pierce my skull and ache for me
to act on them.

maybe
just maybe
if pretend that everything is fine,
the fire will lay low long enough for
me to figure out the next place I'll
hide from my desire to quit entirely.

I hope you write about me

your poems tell us how you really feel,

how you love, how you break and how you deal

I listened from your bedroom and sometimes the stage,

hoping one day I would be

the shining star upon the page.

but the truth is as I write this poem about you,

I don't think you will ever feel the same way I do.

you say you only have your words

so prove it in your songs,

write about how for a moment it was perfect because we

ignored what was wrong.

how I gave you all my trust and time

and when you said, "stop caring so damn much"

I still thought you were a dime.

how I was the most caring and thoughtful person you've

ever met but when I fell for you,

you saw it as a threat.

how you cried to me and I held you in my chest

and when you wanted me to speak to you

I always gave it my best.

how maybe you miss me but you're too scared to say

and when you think about me,

you still feel a certain way.

don't leave out that I understand your struggles

because I have them too,

that makes it hard to lose me

because I know how hard life is to go through.

and even when we ended it I couldn't be mad

because for me nothing can beat what we had.

so yeah for the slim chance you feel the same way,

please mention me when you write

so in your memory I can stay.

red flags will never be beautiful things

you handed me your red flags the day we met

and said they may break me and I stitched them

together to shelter my fears.

I added bows and ribbons to their fabric,

crafted a sweater to wear on our dates,

made a blanket to cover our bodies when

they met in your bed.

I used them to wipe my tears and to

wave away the doubts in my mind.

I tied them around my wrist to hide my scars,

I dyed them colors to match the moonlight

hoping they'd blend in with something beautiful,

but their crimson shade always bled through.

so, your red flags did not break me;

it was my obsession to create art out of warning signs.

my mind

my favorite place to go is a place no one knows,

it's occupied by dark shadows that I make friends with,

they tell me lies about life and how much I'm worth.

a montage of memories plays in the background,

powerful enough to stop me in my tracks.

if I stand still, maybe they'll stay forever.

I invite musicians that play me

ballads about a broken world and

when I'm alone I hum their songs,

desperate for an encore.

hanging on the walls are pictures of paradise

that I painted myself,

featured is a face I use to call home

but I'm not welcome there anymore.

I hide the mistakes behind thick skin

and a smile that says, "I'm okay."

I can let the windows down here

and scream out my struggles or dreams,

they get picked up by the wind

and catch fire when I least expect it.

there's a one way road here that I like to race on,

sometimes I lose because I try to turn back.

this is where I escape to, it's all in my head,

a place where no one knows

and doesn't dare to go.

priorities

the difference between you and me

is that when our house began to burn,

I ran inside to save what we had and

you walked away with the match in your hand.

inbetweeners

they are found when
wounds are fresh from a lost love
and they're affection is needed
for survival of the broken.

they are shiny and new
and fun to play with while
the lonely attempt to feel
full from their touch.

they will lose themselves for you
just to find that their purpose is
to not be loved back but to help
the healing stand tall enough to
walk away.

and they stay put to watch
the person they built fall
for someone as fast as
it took to forget you.

the duality of your hands on my body

it's not that I don't enjoy feeling your palms
on my thighs but sometimes,
they feel like rocks running their sharp
edges on my fragile being and I can't help
but think what we are doing is wrong.
even though I crave the intimacy that
includes your fingers searching for a place
to merge with my frame,
I feel shame set in every time I allow your
reach to bring me pleasure.
I try to treat this exchange as a moment
that disappears with the magic it creates
but I'm always left looking in the mirror
and seeing nothing but an object.

reasons I cry

because most days it's hard to want to be human/ most days it's hard to want to live/ because I can't imagine life after 30/ I can't imagine making it that far/ I cry because I let myself believe when I lost you/ I lost everything/ I cry because I know that's not true/ but either way/ I miss you/ I cry because I'm graduating soon/ I cry because that means life doesn't wait for you to stand up/ it keeps going/ it drags you along whether you like it or not/ I cry because I want out/ I cry because they say it's the little things/ but even the little things/ can't save me/ I cry because I love movies/ I love to escape for a few hours/ I want to drive away and pretend I'm not myself/ that I'm someone I actually want to be/ I cry because at some point/ I have to go back home/ I cry because I have scars on my arm/ they tell me I'm weak/ they tell me I'm not enough for this world/ I cry because it takes my whole body to fight it/ I cry because there are full weeks/ that I truly enjoy living/ that the voices hide away for a while/ but I cry because I know they'll be back

I know they'll be back

on grief

sometimes I'm paralyzed by
the thought of you
and how the place you once
held in my heart is vacant.
I sacrifice so much time to
the hurt that shakes my whole body
when your name echoes in my mind.
I let the memories sit with me because I think,
"how soon is too soon to let go?"

there is no guide to lead me to the person
I will be without you,
so it's easier to idle in the shell of the
person I was but the world moves on
and so will I when I realize that my life
doesn't end with the loss of you.

a prescription capable of altering reality

I bought a new life in a bottle;
placed the pills in my palm and
swallowed hard enough for my
whole body to know something was different.

the seasons changed within a night,
my breath eased with the turning leaves,
bitter cold fell into a colored spring and
the sun peeked through the window with a welcoming
heat.

now my eyes take notice of the little things
that make life beautiful instead of looking
for ways to make each day miserable.
oh, how grateful I am for an entire world
made especially for me.

a part of me

I know I'll go on to kiss a million other faces
and fall in love with half of them.
I'll laugh from conversations about firsts
and try not to wonder where you are.

I know you'll go on to forget about me
and marry someone who loves you half as much.
you'll move away to the city we visited once
and pretend you don't see my name in every street sign.

our time was so small
compared to the many years we'll live;
we'll change with the times
and grow with them too
but that part of me
will always miss that part of you.

head on straight

tilt it upward

and a little to the left

    wait no

       more to the right

move it slowly to

    lock it in place okay now

   shake it to clear the memory and

push down to restart

      there

    now you look sane

30 days without an accident

this is the longest I haven't seen you.
I guess I managed to flush you out
with every tablet I swallow to balance
the chaos you cause.
I constantly look behind my shoulder
to catch you crawling into any crevice
that I've mended from your madness,
but you're not there.
your power still lingers and sometimes
begins to boil,
to which I have not allowed to overflow.
this is the longest I haven't seen you
and often I wonder where you've gone,
but I'm too afraid to find out.

for desire
after kim addonizio

give me a film that allows me to escape,

I want to indulge in its plot so I can hide from my own.

I want grand gestures and serenades made at midnight.

I want the type of love that

only makes sense on the screen.

I want magnetic fights that end in tears falling on your

chest because you still want me after my madness.

I want something *real*.

I want mediocre food at midnight but the friendship

makes up for it,

the one that comes over in a heartbeat

when the other's heart is broken.

give me the girl that carries you across the finish line

when your legs begin to break.

give me tattoos or bracelets,

whatever it takes to show you

how much you mean to me.

give me a life that must be handled with care,

I want nights that cause havoc

but mornings that bring hope.

I want to fall apart sometimes then reassemble my

body to meet mere perfection.

I want to eat all the sweets and regret nothing.

give me beautiful places that ache for me after I've left.

give me all the pain that come with living,

but allow it to mean something at least.

ode to my first love

I believed I could still love you
even though I hated myself
because that was easy to ignore
when I focused on your breath.

you turned my world upside down
and it was fun for a while but
I started to feel sick from hanging
by the thread that you were too scared to cut.

when I told you I had fallen,
you said you didn't feel the same
and I was angry
and broken
and disappointed
and confused

but

I think we can both agree
that we rushed our time together
and it became too intense

for us to handle.

so we parted ways
leaving behind a connection
that grew from touch but
lacked the right communication
to continue without tearing each
other apart.

and although I still miss you,
I'm sure we've both grown since then
but I will always keep a place for you
in between the darkness you brought
and the light you let in.

guardian angels exist on earth

their words make for wings

that guide me through

my darkest nights.

I don't think I'd be here

if they chose not to open

their homes to my madness,

lend their hearts and show me

I'm not alone in this.

so here's to my forever friends,

my family and everyone in my corner,

your open arms are the reason

I've made it this far.

I love you all so much

*I saw your mom at the grocery store
and I didn't say hi*

instead I brushed passed her shoulder to see

if maybe she'd recognize the scent

that came from your room when I stayed the night.

I noticed that she picked up your favorite drink

and now I wonder if you're in town and why

you didn't tell me.

I crossed my arms so she wouldn't notice

that I was wearing your t-shirt,

or maybe I should have stripped it from my body

to give her as a parting gift.

maybe I should have said hello

but would I look any different from

the other girls you brought home?

a glance in her direction would be enough

to remind me that we share this small town

as strangers who once slept in the same bed.

*a stranger asks me what it's like living
with bipolar disorder*
after ari cofer

and I tell them it's more than highs and lows.

it's being grateful for making it one day without
life feeling pointless.
it's being hopeful for days that don't slip from your
memory because your head was spinning too fast.

it's ruling the world and being disappointed as
the leader so you burn everything,
even the beautiful parts.

it's running a marathon only because
your feet won't stop;
chasing a darkness that is guaranteed to come once
you cross the finish line.

it's scary.
it's really really scary.

because some days my head tells me that I'm not enough
for this world and some days
I almost agree with it.

no one brings it up because it's a tough subject but
imagine how tough it is to live
each day inside your head,
constantly looking for a way out so you can enjoy
what's right in front of you.

it takes strength and honesty to battle it.
it takes facing the risk of losing the ones you love
to find yourself.

they ask me what it feels like and
I tell them I wish it were as simple as feeling happy or
sad.

how to run from the mess you made

1. deny the damage
2. pack a small bag containing any pieces left of your spine (it was most likely shattered when you took on the weight of your mistake)
3. begin with a slow jog towards a city that does not have your reputation branded on to the streets
4. fight the tears as you progress; now sprinting past the bridges you burned
5. pause to remember the ruins that remain behind you but
6. never look back

moments when I love being alive

there's a feeling that sets over me
after I've neared the last resort.
my tears begin to tell stories to
my cheeks about how after every
break there is always hope that seeps
through the cracks
and I smile so large I think
the sun shields its rays
because I may be wounded
but I am still here.
I am still here

goodbye

I have reinvented myself,
pulled apart every fiber of my body
to reveal the roots of my suffering;
the origins of my imbalance and
pieced it back together to
create the woman who stands today.

I am composed of patches from
my past life;
from every place I've been,
from everything I've loved,
from every person that's left.

I hold hands with my endings
and guide them alongside me in each
new chapter so they can see:
what's coming is so much better
than what is gone.

"She is a girl who no longer has to avoid the fires of life, because she has learned that she is fireproof. Only people who stand in the fire can know that."

- Glennon Doyle

about the author

Shyanna Mutz is 21 years old, loves movies, coffee and spending hours romanticizing every inch of her life.

Shyanna is a senior history major at Sam Houston State University and plans to continue using her creativity in the public history field. She loves writing, whether it be about her own experiences or about American History. She hopes to write for the rest of her life.
This is her first published piece of work.

keep up with her writing on Instagram:
@shyannawrites

subscribe to her newsletter:
tinyletter.com/lifeofshy

about the illustrator

Patricia M. is a twenty something medical student who enjoys poetry and art and considers the two as her creative outlet. She learned the basics of art and layout design when she worked for their college journal years ago.

keep up with her work on Instagram:
@dolfinne

for business inquiries:
dolfinnebypatricia@gmail.com

acknowledgements

thank you endlessly to my best friend, Jazmin, and my
grandma for being my biggest
supporters through this year of my life.

thank you to my friends and family for loving me
through the pain, even when it was hard to
understand.

thank you to the poetry community I've made online,
this book would not exist without their support.

thank you Patricia for creating such a beautiful cover for
this collection. You made my dreams come to life.

and thank you to my doctors for helping me heal.

it would take a lifetime to explain
how much I love you all.